MINDCRAFT

FAITH-BASED BIBLE STUDIES FOR FAMILIES AND CHILDREN'S MINISTRIES

ADAPTABLE LESSONS FOR VBS & SCHOOLS

Copyright © 2021 AMY TRAURIG & MELISSA SHERIDAN
All Rights Reserved. Printed in the U.S.A.
Published by Two Penny Publishing
850 E Lime Street #266, Tarpon Springs, Florida 34688

No part of this publication may be reproduced, distributed, or transmitted in any form or by any means, including photocopying, recording, or other electronic or mechanical methods, without the prior written permission of the publisher, except in the case of brief quotations embodied in critical reviews and certain other noncommercial uses permitted by copyright law.

For permission requests and ordering information, email the publisher at: info@twopennypublishing.com

For more information about this author or to book event appearance or media interview, please contact the author representative at: info@twopennypublishing.com

Limit of Liability/Disclaimer of Warranty: While the publisher and author have used their best efforts in preparing this book, they made no representations or warranties with respect to the accuracy or completeness of the contents of this book and specifically disclaim any implied warranties of merchantability of fitness for a particular purpose. No warranty may be created of extended by sales representatives or written sales materials. The advice and strategies contained herein may not be suitable for your situation. You should consult with a professional where appropriate. Neither the publisher nor author shall be liable for any loss of profit or any other commercial damages, including but not limited to special, incidental, consequential, or other damage.

**Mind Craft is a 7 Lesson Family & Kids Bible Study
based on a popular game for kids.**

Each lesson gives grown ups and children of all ages Bible based activities and discussions that parallel the experience of getting into the popular pixel building game. From choosing a mode for life to getting out and gaining experiences in your world, by the end of the 7 lessons, we want all gamers to have a deeper grasp on how to build their thoughts on God's truth.

**This lesson package can be read much like an Owner's Manual for a game.
Each lesson is themed with:**

BEFORE YOU BEGIN	Inspirational reads for grown ups
WARRANTY	God's Truth that is tied into discussions
QUEST TIME	Deeper discussions that map out the learning for children
PRAYER - ASSEMBLY REQUIRED	Break down of how participants can pray
OFF SCREEN CHALLENGES	Activate learning by participating in hands-on activities
ONLINE ALTERATION	Virtual options for off screen challenges

TABLE OF CONTENTS

5 LESSON ONE Select Your Mode — Psalm 25:5
WARRANTY: GOD MADE ME TO BE CREATIVE

14 LESSON TWO Gather Resources — Philippians 4:19
WARRANTY: GOD SUPPLIES ALL OF MY NEEDS

23 LESSON THREE Seek Shelter — 1 Corinthians 3:11
WARRANTY: JESUS IS MY FOUNDATION

31 LESSON FOUR Armed for Attacks — 2 Corinthians 10:5
WARRANTY: GOD IS MY GREATEST WEAPON

38 LESSON FIVE Time to Travel — Colossians 3:2
WARRANTY: GOD WILL LEAD ME

46 LESSON SIX Skip Spectator Mode — James 1:22
WARRANTY: IT'S TIME TO START MY FAITH

57 LESSON SEVEN Building Bigger Things — Matthew 6:10
WARRANTY: I COME ALIVE IN GOD'S KINGDOM

67 BONUS: Standing in the Armor
QR code to ORIGINAL SONG for MINDCRAFT

ONE. SELECT YOUR MODE

WARRANTY: GOD MADE ME TO BE CREATIVE

BEFORE YOU BEGIN
A few thoughts from the writers.
This section is for you - the grown ups!
You are welcome to also read with the children.

Did you know that the first version of Minecraft was created in just six days?!? Swedish programmer and designer Markus Persson (aka Notch) set out to create something that would allow for organic exploration and authentic creativity in a virtual world. He began his work on Minecraft on May 10 of that year until May 16 of that same year! The "first version" of Minecraft made its public debut the very next day! Can you imagine creating something in 6 days?!?

> Crazy enough, God's creation story is 6 days too!

In the **beginning** - God started creation
The **first** day - light was created
The **second** day - the sky was created
The **third** day - dry land, seas, plants and trees were created
The **fourth** day - the sun, moon and stars were created
The **fifth** day - creatures that live in the sea and creatures that fly were created
The **sixth** day - animals living on land & humans, made in the image of God, were created
The **seventh** day - God finished His work of creation and rested. Incredible!

Melissa

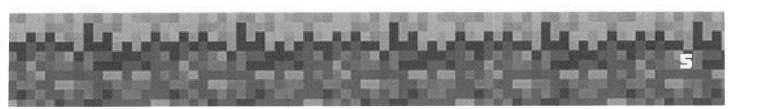

As a child, I loved playing barbies with my little sister. I had always wanted a barbie dream house but did not have one. As an adult, I see how not having the actual pre-made barbie world actually challenged me to be more creative. My little sister and I would spend hours gathering books and bowls from around our house to create our own dream houses for the barbies to live in. I was a huge tomboy and yet I could spend all day gathering resources to build and create worlds for my barbies to live in. There was one problem. After I created the world around the barbies - I was done. My sister would get so mad! She wanted me to stay and interact with the barbies. I always walked away to move on to another toy.

Praise God that He does not treat us like I treated the barbies! God made the world for us to live in and He didn't walk away. He does not get bored with us or give up on us. He delights in interacting with us and providing for us - even today. Though Adam and Eve chose to satisfy the desires of their eyes instead of trusting in God. God still made a way to live with them. God did not allow them to stay in Eden because eating from the tree of life there would have allowed mankind to live countless days in a world now separated from the will of God; the perfect, protected, joy, love and peace-filled world God made for us. Even after they sinned, God showed up and called Adam and Eve to Him.

He knew they sinned against Him and still God pursued them. (**Genesis 3:8**)

Even in their shame, God provided them again with resources and tools.
Who made their first clothes? God did! (**Genesis 3:21**)

They turned their backs on God and yet He found them and cared for them! Do not misunderstand the story of Genesis. This IS God's love story over us. Many Christian scholars believe the "Lord" mentioned in **Genesis 3:8** was Jesus walking to Adam and Eve! God had already started his redemption plan for us. Before we finish the book of Genesis, God is already telling those who seek Him that He is sending someone - to make a way for us to live with Him once again in this world. In this lesson with kids, we will take a look at God's Word that points back to Jesus being God's greatest resource for us! He is the one we need for; beyond the fears, attacks, and limitations of survival mode.

Amy

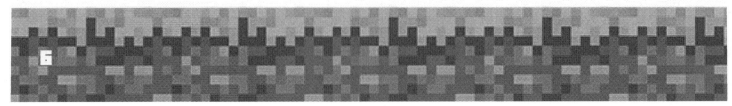

QUEST TIME

Mapping out your quest through question and discussion for kids.

OPERATIONS MANUAL

Let's open up God's Word together and take a look at how the world God created for us can remind us of this popular game. Find time to read the Bible verses below together and dive into the discussions provided OR for younger kids, read the Bible story and skip to the questions.

Minecraft began with only two modes: creative mode and survival mode. Though there are now 5 modes in total, the other modes are based on these two modes.

WHEN SELECTING Creative Mode:

So, you probably know there are different modes in Minecraft. The mode you choose, determines what you will be able to do in your world. In creative mode, you get unlimited resources. Players can fly and have no negative experiences like hunger, hurt, or low health. This mode is created with no enemy mobs to hurt players. I like to think of this as God's intended design for His creation.

READ Genesis 1:26-31; 2:15-22

In the beginning of creating a world....Do you create people or the world for them to live in?

Option: Play Charades. Invite children to act out all the things God made in Genesis 1 while their friends guess what they are pretending to be. In the beginning, God created a world for us to live in! He gave us everything to live an abundant (full) life. What did God create in the beginning for us? (sun, stars, land, water, plants, etc.)

What fun is a world without a person to live in it? Would games be as much fun if you only created the world and not the people? Talk about it.

Why did God make us?

God enjoyed creating the earth and everything in it. Read again **Genesis 1:25.**
Do you think He had some fun making our world like you do when you build in a game?

Created for Creative Mode: You may think that creativity is not for everyone but it's actually fashioned into your DNA. Do you ever wonder how people like Markus create games like Minecraft? It's structured code. To the outside world, it might look like a bunch of letters and numbers, but to the creator, it is specific, unique, precise and intentional.

Only one living thing did God create to be like Him. He blessed them and He said it was VERY GOOD. Read again **Genesis 1:26-31** Human kind!!! God made us like Him. God made us creatively to be creative - just like Him! And He loves us so much that He blessed us. God's intent for creation wasn't chaos. It was creativity. To anyone else you may appear to just be another person but to your Creator you are specifically made, uniquely loved, with precise and intentional purpose!

WHEN SELECTING Survival Mode:

In survival mode, all players are able to gather materials and tools to build and craft items. Unlike creative mode, players now experience health issues, hunger pains, loss of armor and breath as their oxygen bars go down. In survival, you have to earn your achievements and it's up to you to collect your own resources. Survival mode reminds me of life after Adam and Eve sinned. When they listened to the enemy instead of God, our world became one in survival mode.

READ Genesis 3:1-24

Who met Eve in the Garden?

What did the snake say to Eve?

Like Eve, the enemy will often get us to question why we are trusting God. The sneaky snake was able to gain Eve's trust by getting her to question her trust in God. How does the enemy do this to us today? *Leaders and parents can share a personal story.*

When we stop trusting in God, we switch modes in life. Eve switched modes. How did life change for Adam and Eve after they ate the fruit? Re-read **Genesis 3:7-24.**

They were ashamed	vs.7
They hid from God	vs.8
They were afraid of God	vs.10
They lied to God	vs.12-13
They lost trust in each other	vs.12-13
The woman is cursed	vs.16
The man is cursed	vs.17
They can no longer live forever with God	vs. 22-24

When Adam and Eve lost sight of why they were created (to see God's glory, live with him, and live out a life where others see Him glorified), they chose their glory over God's. And when we lose sight of why we are created we choose our way over His, it's like choosing survival mode over creative mode. Like the game, there is death, attacks of enemies (creepers), and it's up to us to work to survive.

But Jesus came to redeem our survival mode! Not in a "we will never have trials or attacks of the enemy here on earth kind of way," but in a "connected back to the creator and not alone kind of way." Plus eternity was secured at the cross for those who believe. We are going to learn more about Jesus next time. So remember, even when satan tries to get you to lose sight of what God created you for - because of Jesus, the game is won and we can return to the life we were made for!

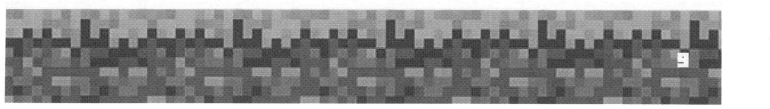

1. What was your favorite part of the Bible story?

2. Who made Adam and Eve? Who made you?

3. Did God have big plans for Adam and Eve? Does God have big plans for you?

4. How is the Garden of Eden like MineCraft?

5. How is creative mode different from survival mode?

6. Why did Adam and Eve have to leave the Garden of Eden?

7. Do you ever find yourself losing sight of what God might be wanting you to do?

8. Are there ever times when you cannot stop thinking about what you want to do over what God wants you to do? *Example: maybe you are mad at a friend but God wants you to forgive. Maybe you took something that wasn't yours and God wants you to give it back.*

9. Choose today, what mode do you want to choose? Talk about it together.

PRAYER: ASSEMBLY REQUIRED

Building up our minds by breaking down one Bible verse and praying it together.

STEP 1:
Read **Psalms 25:5** together.
Read **Psalms 25:5** in different "modes" like quiet as a mouse mode,
slow like a turtle mode, fast forward mode (fast), rewind mode (read backward)...etc.

STEP 2:
How can God's truth GUIDE your mind in TRUTH?

STEP 3:
Take time to listen to God. Close your eyes and try and clear out every distraction in your mind. Ask God what He wants to TEACH you.

STEP 4:
Declare together: God you are our GOD! You are our SAVIOR!

STEP 5:
In what ways do you try to do life without God? How can we put our HOPE in him all day long?

STEP 6:
Pray together **Psalms 25:5** out loud. Invite God to do STEPS 1-5 in our minds this week

OFF SCREEN CHALLENGES

Troubleshooting what you are learning; interactive activities for real life mode together.

1. SUPPLIES: paper, pencils, markers, crayons for off screen challenge

Draw out a map of your life. Incorporate key moments that have happened that have either challenged you or things you've accomplished so far. The map can have some of your low points or high points. Give students some personal examples. Include in your map where you want to go. It's important to note that the enemy wants to remind us of our past and God wants to redeem us of our future in Him. Once you create your unique life map, don't forget to have your parent or ministry director capture a pic and share it with us! Don't forget to tag us and hashtag #MINDcraft. We can't wait to see what you come up with!

2. SUPPLIES: blindfold, items around the house as "obstacles," cookies

Play "follow the leader" 3 or 4 times. For older kids, take turns blindfolding each other AND add "obstacles" for them to avoid while following the directions the "leader" calls out. Play the game a few more times but this time, tell the person who has to follow the leader that they have a choice: If they follow the leader, they win the game and can keep playing. If they walk on their own to the cookie they can eat and taste the cookie but then they have to sit in time out for 1 minute. After you play sit and talk about it.

> When was it easy to follow the leader?
> When was it hard to follow the leader?
> Was it ever hard to trust the leader?

Adam and Eve followed God until they chose to go off on their own and eat the one fruit He told them not to eat. They chose to disobey instead of trusting God's direction. Because they disobeyed, all of mankind had to live in a "time out" from God. God used to walk and talk and spend time with them in the Garden. Because of their sin, Adam and Eve and every person born after them was cursed and could no longer live in the love and best-friendship with God; the life God created for them. Sadness, fear, and loneliness were introduced into their lives because they obeyed their selfish sin. Do you ever experience Sadness, fear, and loneliness? Are you ever tempted to disobey God and trust your selfish sinful wants?

God sent Jesus to make a "way" back to Him; away from the sin that separated us from Him. (Have you ever heard the song "WayMaker?" It's about Jesus!) God loves you so much, that He did not want to stay away from you forever so He provided " a way" through Jesus. When we follow Him, God can live within us (Holy Spirit) AND God promises that even after death we can be with Him again! There will be no sadness, badnessm fear, and loneliness in Heaven!
Do you know anyone else with that power or that much love for you?!

ONLINE ALTERATION: If you are playing with a group of kids who are not in the room with you, alter the game. Play "Simon Says" on the screen instead of "Follow the Leader." Invite kids to get a cookie treat from their house and set it next to them as they play. Give them the choice to keep playing with you or to eat the cookie and sit alone or with their screen off. Continue with the conversation.

3. SUPPLIES: items around you

If you are playing with kids in a room, select 8 supplies and hide them around the room for children to find them as you call them out. Call out items for children to find: socks, pencils, cups... etc. Once you have called around 6 items for the children to find, then gather together and give them 2 minutes to create a person or a structure.

Once you are finished, invite children to share their creations! Ask them how this game reminds them of mindcraft? How would the game be different if they were in survival mode?

For older kids, play again. This time you are in survival mode. Add 2 more supplies they are able to gather for this "mode" of the game. As children gather supplies, call out "attacks" where children have been attacked by mobs and have to then build and gather with only one arm or some of their supplies are stolen. Once they have gathered what they can, invite them to build NOT for 2 minutes but for as long as they can hold their breath. (remind them of the consequences that come from playing in "survival mode."

Once you are done ask what was different about each game mode? How is this game like our life? God created us to be creative and find joy in creating and caring for everything in the world around us. What gets in the way of our joy? What gets in the way of our creativity?

ONLINE ALTERATION: If you are playing with a group of kids who are not in the room with you, invite them to find the items you call out that are around them.

TWO. GATHER RESOURCES

WARRANTY: GOD SUPPLIES ALL OF MY NEEDS

BEFORE YOU BEGIN
This section is for you - the grown ups!
You are welcome to also read with children.

READ Philippians 4:19. What does this verse tell us about God? What resources does He give us? Did you know the enemy comes to give you the exact opposite? In John 10:10, Jesus says the thief (satan) comes only to steal and kill and destroy; I (Christ) have come that you may have life, and have it in full.

I remember how angry my son was after spending a good hour building this awesome house on Minecraft only to have it wrecked by the monsters of the night. I asked him "well how did they get in your house?" He said, "I accidentally left the door open." I thought to myself, how often, in our spiritual lives do we give the enemy access or we aren't prepared or equipped for the darkness? **Ephesians 4:27** says "Don't give the devil a foothold," which means don't give him the opportunity or accessibility to your life.

READ Ephesians 6:10-18

The armor isn't so much about your stance against evil but more your trust and posturing toward God. Your victory in spiritual warfare was actually secured at the cross **(Rev. 12:11)**. The problem is, we can lose sight of the cross and rely on our own strength. The full armor of God is what protects you when you have doubt, guilt or fear. The way you stand against the accusations of the devil is to believe what God's Word says about you instead of the lies of the enemy. Don't get it twisted, the enemy is after your house, your stuff, the things you've built, your gifts and talents. If you give him an open door or access, he will take it as an opportunity to destroy you. Just like the game gives you survival steps to do before nighttime arrives like, building shelter, crafting tools and weapons, securing valuables, etc., the Bible gives you survival steps to protect your life from the enemy.

Melissa

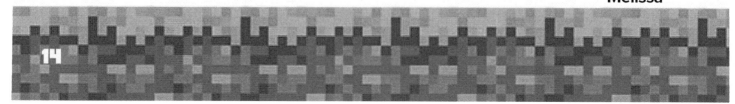

When Melissa first mentioned the idea of creating a curriculum based on this popular game I was excited at the impact it could have on children. Little did I know, just how much the truths in this study would impact me!

Let's take this lesson about resources, for example. Did you know that in these games, the rarest resources (and equipment) are found in the depths? If you want the rarest resource of wood, you have to travel to the depths of the water biomes for sunken ships. My ten year old son has also encouraged me to trust him and travel deep into the bedrock to gather it as a rare resource. Grown ups, are you still with me? God wants to take us deeper! Inviting God to take the lead in our lives is the beginning of our greatest adventures. He desires to take us to deeper levels so we can gain deeper healing and heavenly resources of revelation, healing, love, joy, and so much more!

In these games each player is able to check their inventory. This inventory displays the resources available as well as those you are running out of. Take a moment to take inventory in your life. What resources are you running low on? God loves you so much that He didn't leave you in this world to fend for yourself alone. Melissa and I pray that through these devotions and activities you will be able to go switch from a world where you survive into a life filled with the fullness of God where you thrive!

Amy

QUEST TIME

Mapping out your quest through question and discussion for kids

OPERATIONS MANUAL

Let's open up God's Word together and take a look at how God gives us resources to live. Find time to read the Bible verses below together and dive into the discussions provided OR for younger kids, read the Bible story below and skip to the questions.

Last week we learned that God created the world to be in community with us. He created all of its resources for us to live and thrive in His goodness and glory. Even when sin changed our mode, God didn't change His mode of love for us.

> In games, why do you collect resources and create tools?

What are some resources players can gather in games? (coal, iron, gold, diamonds, wood, crops...etc.)

How do players collect resources? (mining, farming, chopping, interacting with others...etc.)

What can you create with these resources? (example: collect the resource cobblestone to craft a furnace, or use wood to build a crafting table)

In **Genesis 1** we read about how God spent the first 6 days of creation creating resources for us to live, survive and thrive. What resources did God create for us in Genesis 1?

Option: Play *Follow the Leader*. Have you ever played "Follow the Leader?" When you play, who are you focused on? Why? When we follow God, we are better able to see the many resources He has already given to us. Can we see God's resources if we are not following Him? Let's take a look at some of the resources God wants to provide us with!

Jesus is our greatest resource! We can use the fun images and ideas from our apps and games to explain: ***When we "mine" (dig deeper) into God's word we will find more of God's resources for our lives!***

We can ask God's Holy Spirit to help us to find the resources he has placed throughout the Bible. He can also help us collect resources from other wise followers of Christ- just like we can collect resources from other players in the game! Read **1 Corinthians 2:6-10**

Did you know that when God made you He placed resources inside you?!
What are some dreams you have? What do you love to do? God made you and put dreams and abilities in you. We can ask His Holy Spirit to help "draw out" the dreams God put deep within us. Read **Proverbs 20:5**

Trusting in God is like harvesting a good crop Read **Matthew 13:18-23**

Trusting Jesus is like laying a firm foundation Read **1 Corinthians 3:11**

Following Jesus will help us mine for treasures Read **Colossians 2:3**

God's word is a lamp so I can see where I am going Read **Psalm 119:105**

What about resources like (water) **John 4:10-14** (iron) **Proverbs 27:17**?

Option: Play *Hot Potato* but use bread instead of a potato to play When you collect the resource "wheat," what can craft? Bread. How does bread help players in a game? It gives lives and health. The Bible calls Jesus our "bread of life." What does this mean? We still eat breakfast, lunch and dinner so how do we "feast on Jesus" as "bread of life?" Read **John 6:29-37** and **Matthew 4:4**.

Jesus is the most important resource God gives us! Just like we talked about earlier, we can find this resource only when we choose to follow God. If we choose to follow someone or something else we will miss the life changing resource of Jesus! Can you find more Bible verses about resources God gives us on your own? Let us know and tag us on social media **#MindCraft**.

FOR OLDER KIDS: *Have you ever heard someone say "I could just eat you up?" What did they mean? When we adore someone and long for them it can feel like seeing a donut through a donut shop window and longing to get close to the donut and consume it so we feel full and satisfied. Jesus as our "bread of life" does not mean we literally eat him. When we take communion we eat pieces of bread that remind us of Him being this bread of life for us. Jesus says, when we adore him and long for Him, He will satisfy us more than anything we could long to eat. Eating food is necessary to life. Following Jesus will restore us and give us eternal life- much like bread in minecraft helps gain life and health.*

BONUS Bible Trivia:

Did you know Jesus was a carpenter? Well his dad Joseph was a carpenter. According to Jewish tradition, all sons were trained in the career paths of their father. So, we can safely assume Jesus was a carpenter too. What's a carpenter? Well, what do you call someone who builds things from wood?

Now let's think back to your apps and games- In order to build many of the tools, players first have to collect wood and build a crafting table. You cannot create many items without this table. Essentially, every player must become a carpenter in order to begin creating - as they are intended to in their world.

> *"Jesus left there and went to his hometown, accompanied by His disciples. When the Sabbath came, He began to teach in the synagogue, and many who heard Him were amazed. "Where did this man get these things?" they asked. "What's this wisdom that has been given to Him? What are these remarkable miracles He is performing? Isn't this the carpenter?" Matthew 6:1-3.*

The more we become like Jesus Christ, the more creative we can become! God gave us Jesus, to make a way for us to live as His sons and daughters. He does not want us to live under the curse we received because of sin Remember the curses from Genesis 3? Jesus redeemed the curse. Read Galatians 3:13-14

When we give our lives to Jesus, we can live with Him and truly tap into the creativity God has placed within us! Jesus, the carpenter, is our greatest resource! Read John 14:6

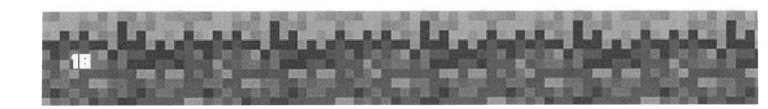

While minecraft is a game about building a world different from the one you live in- the tools God gives us are to build us up for the world we do live in.

1. How can we be carpenters like Jesus?

2. How can we eat the bread of life today?

3. After reading through **Ephesians 6:10-18** about the armor of God, how equipped do you feel you are spiritually? Would you say you protect your valuables more on Minecraft than in your spiritual life. Your heart and mind would be valuables.

4. How can we protect our minds?

5. How can we protect our hearts?

6. How does God's armor help us on our quests in school? At home? With friends?

PRAYER: ASSEMBLY REQUIRED

Building up our minds by breaking down one Bible verse and praying it together.

STEP 1:
Read **Philippians 4:19**

STEP 2:
Common NEEDS are: safety, rest, food & water, health, and relationships. Talk about the difference between a need and a want. We all have physical needs and emotional needs. Think about 5 things you NEED right now.

STEP 3:
How many names do you have? (share first names, middle names and nicknames you all have) Did you know that one of God has MANNNNYYY names? One of His names actually means "Provider"! Say His name together: Jehovah Jirah. This name for God actually means "The Lord Will Provide" or "Provider". You can see this name in **Genesis 22:14**.

STEP 4:
Can God ever run out of anything? Are there any "supplies" God can run out of? NO! **Philippians 4:19** reminds us that our God wants to open up His riches- that never run out- to supply what we need! What does that tell you about God? (He is powerful, rich, loving, generous...etc.)

STEP 5:
Worship God together! Spend 1 minute quietly together. Invite the children to open their hearts and minds to be empty of any worry, want or other thought. Invite them to talk to God. Tell Him your needs with your hearts and minds. We can thank God before we ever see something change because we know who God is: Jehovah Jirah. Thank Him for being your Provider. Ask Him to open your mind and heart to hear Him this week and see His mighty hand supplying riches into your life! He has great resources for you.

OFF SCREEN CHALLENGES

Troubleshooting what you are learning; interactive activities for real life mode together.

1. SUPPLIES: paper, pencils, markers, crayons for off screen challenge

This week we want to see you draw up the ideal armor of God on a character that you design. Make sure he/she is equipped with all the pieces mentioned in **Ephesians 6:10-18.** Once you create your unique character with armor, don't forget to have your parent or ministry director capture a pic and share it with us!

Don't forget to tag us and hashtag **#MINDcraft.** We can't wait to see what you come up with!

2. SUPPLIES: water, bowl, tiny toys, hammer

Find small toys and place them in a bowl. Fill the bowl with water. Once the water is frozen put the bottom of the bowl under warm water. This warm water will loosen the bowl shaped ice cube. Bring the ice cube outside and invite children to use their tools to find the hidden "resources" you have frozen in the ice. As you play, review the bible stories and questions you talked about earlier.

ONLINE ALTERATION: Follow the steps above but demonstrate it on camera. As you use your tools ask the children what they think is hidden in the ice cube. Maybe try and use some tools that won't work first and see how the students react.

How is hammering the ice cube like mining in minecraft?

What is the best resource they have ever found in the game?

What is the greatest resource God has given us?

3. SUPPLIES: paper, books, coloring items, glue/tape (optional)

Go for a walk and search for "resources." Invite children to find leaves and wood and rocks. As you discover these resources get creative and think of ways to turn the resources into tools. As you find leaves and flowers, take them home and put them in between two pieces of paper. Place the paper inside a large book to flatten your leaf or flower. Use the leaves and papers to create "clothing." You might even choose to draw pictures of people and glue or tape your findings on them as clothing. (Even though in **Genesis 3:21** it says God used animal skin to clothe man and women, we won't use animal skin today.)

ONLINE ALTERATION: Invite children to take 60 seconds and jump off the camera to head outside with parent permission. Ask them to find 2 or 3 items. When they come back on screen show what you all found. Using your imagination, try and think of tools you could build with what you found.

What tools do you think Adam and Eve built?

If you were a carpenter like Jesus, what would you make?

> Take time to thank God for making you creative! Thank Him for making a world for us to explore and create in!

THREE. SEEK SHELTER

WARRANTY: JESUS IS MY FOUNDATION

BEFORE YOU BEGIN
This section is for you - the grown ups!
You are welcome to also read with the children.

I really wanted to use jello somewhere in this lesson. I just love the idea of trying to build something on jello. My kids love it as a snack but it would be the worst foundation. Doesn't it seem ironic that this same logic is how many grown ups build our foundation? We take things we love, people we love, and truths that seem good to use (like a sweet snack) and we make them foundational in us. I love my husband but if I make him the foundational source of my affirmation, I will always need more from him. It's a shaky foundation. I love wine and chocolate too but if they become the foundational source of my joy then I find myself on a slippery slope. In the same way, jello can be a fun snack but a terrible foundation. I would also like to point out that jello made a great office staple holder in one of my all time favorite tv shows.

I digress... My point is, while God created a world where we can find many sources of happiness, laughter, and wonderful feelings, He gave us only one foundation we should build our lives on. Jesus. When we choose to believe that Jesus is the Son of God sent for us, we see God's love for us personified in this Savior. We see the gift of grace that Jesus is for us. He came for us without any prerequisites or applications. As for me and my house, the foundation is falling in love with Jesus Christ every day. He is the source of my hope. He is the source I turn to for help. He guards my mind when I text and who I cling to when I am lonely. Knowing He loves me, never leaves me, that he died for me, and overcame death for me, satisfies deeper than any glass of cabernet of human affirmation. This foundation has brought my household through the toughest storms and enemy attacks.

As for me and my house, we will praise the Lord {our firm foundation}. Adapted **Joshua 24:15**

Amy

QUEST TIME

Mapping out your quest through question and discussion for kids

OPERATIONS MANUAL

In popular building app games, you have the option to build on flat or infinite ground. One of the first things you do in your game is find the perfect environment to build a shelter. Where you begin your build and what you build the foundation from will determine if you can survive storms and attacks. The same is true with where and what we build our thoughts on. In Jesus, we find our greatest shelter and the best ground to build our foundation on. Let's take a look.

STEP 1: READ **Matthew 7:24-27** or **Luke 6:46-49**

STEP 2: Choose where you build

What is Jesus saying about the importance of WHERE you build?

What is an environment? (the surroundings in which a person, animal, or plant lives or operates.)

> Did you know, God is our Shelter? He can protect us in times of trouble.

READ Psalm 91:1-2

We are going to take a look at how to dwell (or live) with God as our shelter! There is one BIG verb in Psalm 91 that gives away how we can begin to build... did you see what word it is? TRUST.

> When we trust in God, we begin to build our thoughts based on faith in Him.
> This is the best environment to build anything.

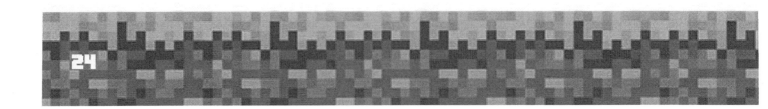

FOR OLDER KIDS: *Stop and think: What types of thoughts are you having right now? The thoughts you keep can tell you a lot about your "environment." For example: Are you thinking about fears right now? Worries? Are you anxious or filled with hope?*

Option: Draw a picture of what thoughts you have in your mind right now. Share. God is perfect love. The Bible says, where God is put in charge (made Lord), we find freedom from darkness, fears, and any unloving thoughts.

Read 2 Corinthians 3:17 & 1 John 4: 18

What does this mean for us today? If we invite God in to take charge of our thoughts, He promises to create an environment of hope, joy, peace, that is filled with infinite resources only a loving Creator can give us!

When talking about building a foundation on Jesus, we begin in our mind.

Read Colossians 3:2

> "Setting our minds on things above" means that God wants us to craft our minds to think about His resources.

STEP 3: Evaluate your environment

What is your environment?

Are there things you cannot control in your environment? What are some things you can control?

Some things in your life, you don't have much control over; like who your family is, but there are certain things that you can control. You can control what you choose to think about, who you choose to think about, and how you think about yourself, God, and others.

What types of environments do you find in your games? We are going to talk about today from your game are flat ground and infinite ground. Flat ground is best for building in creative mode where you don't need to find resources. In survival mode, infinite ground is best because it has different resources and types of ground. Down low you have lakes, trees, and fish. Up on higher ground, there are mining resources and snow.

Remember our first lesson where we talked about creative mode being a lot like the Garden of Eden? God was with Adam and Eve in the beginning (before sin). Just like using flat ground in creative mode, they didn't have to go out and look for shelter. God had created the perfect environment for them to build.

For survival mode, the resources we need are not always easy to find. When we follow God, He will help us find the resources we need to build. He leads us to the infinite ground that gives us the foundation we need and the perfect environment for us to build our thoughts, dreams and desires on. So WHAT or WHO is our infinite foundation?

STEP 4: Choose your foundation to begin building

Read **1 Corinthians 3:11**

WHAT you build with matters too! Remember how we talked about Jesus being our greatest resource?! There are countless building blocks in games for building but are all of them good for building houses? Would you lay a foundation of wool or build walls of sponge, sand or TNT? Building a shelter from TNT is like building thoughts on worry. They are going to blow up at some point under the fire of circumstances!

Jesus is our greatest resource because He is the only one we can build our shelter on. A shelter that will stand against any enemy's attacsk, invasion, or storm! God didn't give up on us when we entered survival mode! He loves us so much that he gave us Jesus!

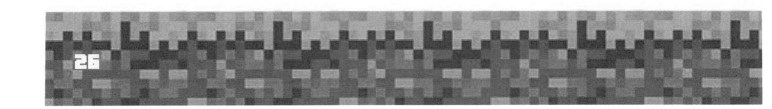

1. So what tools can we use to build a strong foundation of faith?

2. When you think about your life with Jesus Christ: what do you picture your faith "house" looking like? *Maybe draw a picture of what it looks like and the areas that you could improve your faith.*

3. How can you choose Jesus this week?

4. How can you make Him the foundation for your thoughts?

> We can craft our minds to be like Christ!
> He is our solid foundation who gives us
> His Holy Spirit as our best friend to
> help us through any challenge!

FOR OLDER KIDS: *Go back to Colossians 3:2*

What are the earthly things this verse says are not a good foundation for our thoughts? (worries, doubts and fears that only affect our life on earth). Share personal stories. What "resources" can we fix our minds on that come from above? (Jesus and his hope, the Presence of His Holy Spirit with us, love and other "truths" we know about God but may not always see in our earthly environments). Share personal stories.

Choose how you build & continue reading Colossians 3:1-3. Paul is speaking about HOW you build. Why is HOW you build important? Have you ever demolished a character in your game in order to build a new one?

> Before you and I can be built into new characters in Christ -
> we first have to go through demolition!

PRAYER: ASSEMBLY REQUIRED

Building up our minds by breaking down one Bible verse and praying it together.

STEP 1:
Read **1 Corinthians 3:11**

STEP 2:
How many foundations does this verse tell us there are? What does that mean?
If we try to build a shelter for our hearts and minds on anything that is not Jesus, it will fall down.

STEP 3:
Identify what a shelter is? The place we run to for safety, hope, and help.

STEP 4:
What are examples of things we put in place of Jesus as the foundation for our shelters?

Here is an example: MONEY: When money is where we find shelter, what will happen to us when we run out of money? Or when we lose a job? Our shelter falls!

STEP 5:
Unlike money, we will never run out of Jesus! Having money sometimes can change how we trust other people. It can change our hearts to be selfish. Jesus changes our hearts to be courageous, filled with love, hope, and help people. Jesus is the one foundation the enemy cannot knock down! He can shelter us, hold us, and help us from anything that comes into our environments!

STEP 6:
Pray together. Take 1 minute of quiet to teach children to listen to God. Ask God to remind you of a time He was there for you as a shelter? After the minute is up, pray together and thank God for being the 1 foundation we can find shelter in-
no matter what!

OFF SCREEN CHALLENGES

Troubleshooting what you are learning; interactive activities for real life mode together.

1 SUPPLIES: scrap paper, pencils, markers, glue, miscellaneous building supplies (such as popsicle sticks, cardboard) for off screen challenge

This week let's build your "faith" house out of fun materials you can find outside and around the house! Get creative! Once you build your unique house, don't forget to have your parent or ministry director capture a pic and share it with us!

ONLINE ALTERATION: Invite children to gather playing cards or pieces of paper. Give them 60 seconds to "build their house". Show off your houses when you are done.

Talk about how ground makes a good location to build and what makes for a poor foundation for our builds? Review our Bible verses from this lesson.

2 SUPPLIES: towels, hats, props, and blankets

Choose one person to be the group's character. Explain that you have gathered resources for everyone to dress their character with. Have this person stand with arms stretched out. Invite the rest of the group to "dress" the character with all the supplies. Pile them on! Then instruct the character to go on a quest and hop to the other side of the room. Repeat with another child being a new character.

Ask what made the quest difficult?

Read **Hebrews 12:1**

What hindered the character on their quest?
Would taking off the towels and blankets have made it easier?
Sometimes we carry old thoughts, fears, and worries that Jesus wants us to let go of so we can "run our race" or quest with Him!
What thoughts can we shed so we can fully trust Jesus with our minds?

ONLINE ALTERATION: As a leader piles on the towels, hats, and blankets. Give an example of trying to accomplish a chore while wearing them. OR if you are in a small space. Pile on each item as children name "old thoughts" that hinder us from trusting Jesus. Talk about how silly you look and how much easier it would be to lay EVERYTHING we are carrying down at Jesus' feet!

3 SUPPLIES: Sand, beach toys

Work with children to create sand castles. As you work, ask the children what kinds of castles they are building. Talk about what they build in games like Minecraft. What foundations are good to build on in their games? What foundations are bad? Is sand a good foundation?

Review **Matthew 7:24-27** or **Luke 6:46-49**

There are a lot of blocks we can use in minecraft but not all of them are made for foundation and walls. When you try and lay a foundation other than Christ in your life it is like building on sand! But it is important to note that even a house that feels ruined can be redeemed and re-built in Christ. God LOVES you and wants to bring restoration to your life. But He can't help you if you are unwilling to accept His help.

FOUR. ARMED FOR ATTACKS

WARRANTY: GOD IS MY GREATEST WEAPON

BEFORE YOU BEGIN
This section is for you - the grown ups!
You are welcome to also read with the children.

My 6 year old son had built this incredible mansion on Minecraft. It had a glass pool, and a library, a rooftop bedroom overlooking the hills. He switched to survival mode and had accidentally left the door open to his house. Sadly, a creeper got in and destroyed his house. I don't think it's a coincidence that most of the evil things in the game thrive in the night.

Think about it... Phantoms, Mobs and Zombies spawn in the night or in a thunderstorm. **John 10:10** says the enemy comes like a thief to steal and destroy.

Just like we discussed in lesson one, it's important to remember that a life in Christ is not free from trouble or trials. The stronger we are in Christ, the harder the enemy has to try. Did you know in hard mode on Minecraft, the enemy is able to break down doors to attack? They don't even wait for an opening. That's crazy! But we can be confident in Christ that He will provide, sustain and help us persevere through whatever life throws at us. The Bible says that we must put on the armor of God to help us stand against the attacks of the enemy. Each piece protects and leads us to victory. The great thing is that when we give our life to Christ we don't have to fight for victory but from it! We are victorious because of Christ!

Melissa

QUEST TIME

Mapping out your quest through question and discussion

OPERATIONS MANUAL

Let's open up God's Word together and take a look at how God is our greatest weapon! God gives us victory against the enemy's attacks through Jesus. Because of Jesus, we can be filled with His Holy Spirit who destroys every enemy thought that attacks us!

> Before we begin let's talk about WHO the enemy is!

Our entire study, MindCraft, is about focusing our minds on our faith. Today we are going to look at how satan uses enemy attacks to try and defeat our thoughts. The enemy attacks like:

A thief in the night: READ **John 10:10**
With flaming arrows: READ **Ephesians 6:16**
A roaring lion: READ **1 Peter 5:8**

There are so many more verses about how satan disguises himself and comes to attack us but these are the three we will focus on. In our games, there are also enemies that attack. These enemies can be: zombies, skeletons, monsters or creepers. Can you think of any more? *Have the students share.*

Read **John 10:10**

What does this verse say about the enemy? When does he attack?
What does he try to steal? What does this verse say about God?

In our games, monsters attack and cause the most damage in the dark of night.
Do you find yourself scared more in the daylight or in darkness?

Did you know: In the game, enemies burn up in the light? A single torch gives enough light to prevent monsters from spawning completely within a 7 block range. It reminds me of a verse in John chapter 3, where Jesus is saying that everyone who does wicked things hates the light and does not come to the light, because their work would be exposed. Jesus is the light of the world **(John 8:12).** So if we remain in Him, we will reflect His light. If we don't remain in Christ, we are susceptible to our sinful desires. Here are some more fun verses about light: **Psalm 27:1, Psalm 119:105, Psalm 18:28.** *You can have the kids read the verses and every time they hear certain words (like light and dark) use a light to turn on and off.*

FOR OLDER KIDS: *Read Matthew 5:16 How can God's light shine through me and help others who may be in "dark" times?*

Read Luke 11:34-35 What does this verse say about your eyes? Can what you look at affect your thoughts/mind? Can what you look at affect if your emotions/heart and fill you with light or darkness? How can we invite God's light into our mind/heart this week by focusing on Him?

In the survival mode game, you have to face zombies, spiders, creepers, and skeletons many times. Each creature requires you to have a unique fighting style in order to defeat it. What are the spiritual mobs or skeletons in your closet in your own life? How can God help you to defeat their attacks? Some days we can feel like we are the target of an attack. We may decide to have a good day but every thought that enters our mind and transfers to our heart becomes a belief. What are you believing and is it in alignment with what God's truth about you? Share a personal story if you have one.

Read Ephesians 6:16 What stands out to you about this verse? Who is shooting the arrows? What did you notice about the arrows? Who are they aimed at? The enemy AIMS at you! Why? The enemy (satan) knows you are so loved by God and he hates God. Satan does whatever he can to get us to turn our backs on each other and God. He does NOT want your mind to be focused on God's Truth. If you and I knew all the time just how amazing God was and how incredible His love for us was- satan could not stand a chance! Even in this popular game, flaming arrows are sent to attack us! Even their arrows will hurt or even kill you!

Read **1 Peter 5:8**
What does this tell you about the enemy? What does this tell you about your mind?

Remember that first verse from **John 10:10**? The enemy doesn't come to just steal one thing, he wants to take everything! He wants to devour everything God has in our life like a hungry lion attack! But there is good news! God does not leave us to stand against the enemy alone.

> **John 10:10** reminds us that God gives us life to the fullest!
>
> **Ephesians 6:16** reminds us that when we hold onto our faith we will be shielded from the attacks!
>
> **Ephesians 6:11** reminds us that God gives us armour that can stand against any attack.
>
> And **Psalm 27:1** reminds us that with Jesus as the light in our life- we have nothing to fear!
>
> Bonus verse: **1 John 4:4** this is one of our favorites! Here we are reminded that there is no enemy in our world who is stronger than the Holy Spirit living in us.

Do not let the enemy stay one more minute. Kick out his lies! Hold up your shield of faith. Call on the name of Jesus because His Spirit is within every believer and is ready to take down every enemy attack! *We have provided a song that goes along with this curriculum to help students learn the armor of God in a fun way! Take some time to let the kids learn it and put some fun arm movements with it! See page 68 for a link to this brand new song!*

FOR OLDER KIDS: *Did you know that in the game, if you build a bed the night will go faster? How does this relate to our faith? Read Psalm 4:8 & Exodus 33:14 & Isaiah 26:3. What do these verses tell you?*

Much like building a bed is to give your character rest, building a resting place in Jesus will protect you. The dark times will not seem as long when we rest in the One who loves us and is with us through it all. How can God be where you find rest this week? Read **Matthew 11:28-30**

Pray for each other.

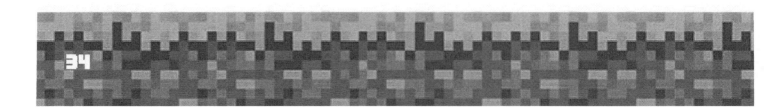

PRAYER: ASSEMBLY REQUIRED

Building up our minds by breaking down one Bible verse and praying it together.

STEP 1:
Read Read **2 Corinthians 10:5**

STEP 2:
What does it mean to bring every thought into captivity?
Taking every thought captive requires faith in God and a turning from sin. It requires us to take inventory of what we think about. Take some time this week to write out a thought inventory. Reflect on areas of thought that maybe need reframed with the truth and grace of Jesus Christ.

STEP 3:
Read **2 Thessalonians 3:3.**
It's important to remember that the Lord is faithful and He will strengthen us and protect us from the enemy. Take time to pray for God's strength and not your own.

STEP 4:
Read **1 Peter 5:8-9.**
What does it mean to have a sober mind?
Take a piece of paper and try to draw eyes and a cross with your eyes closed. The picture doesn't look as good as it would have if we had our eyes opened. The same is true in our spiritual life. If we aren't alert to the attacks of the enemy it's going to be hard to keep our eyes on the cross. Pray for God to alert your heart, mind and spirit to what is good & what isn't good.

STEP 5:
READ **James 4:7**
We have to first submit ourselves to God, to then, be able to resist the devil. A lot of times we try and operate in our own strength or we go to something else first instead of God. Think about the things that you might go to before you go to God. Talk about them. Why do you go there first? Pray for God to help you to submit to Him first.

OFF SCREEN CHALLENGES

Troubleshooting what you are learning; interactive activities for real life mode together.

SUPPLIES: paper, pencils, markers, crayons for off screen challenge

Draw a picture of what your enemy looks like. If you have trouble with anger, maybe your enemy is a fiery creature. If you have trouble with laziness, maybe your enemy casts spells to put you to sleep. Once you draw out your enemy, think of two ways you can work to defeat him. Part of overcoming sin in our life is, first, acknowledging that it's there and second, coming up with a plan to help get rid of it. Once you build your enemy, if you feel comfortable, share them with your group/class/parent and don't forget to have your parent or ministry director capture a pic and share it with us!

Don't forget to tag us and hashtag **#MINDcraft.** We can't wait to see what you come up with!

SUPPLIES: *none*

Play *London Bridge*. Take turns being the bridge and being the children who walk through the bridge. You may even choose to replace the lyrics with:

> "Jesus can take every thought, every thought, every thought.
> Jesus can take every thought. Ev-Ry- thought!"

This game can serve as a great reminder that we should not let a thought go by without letting Jesus hold it captive. (The bridge representing Jesus and the people representing thoughts.) When you're playing a few rounds talk about **2 Corinthians 10:5**. How can we give Jesus every thought? What are some lies, doubts, fears, or emotions you have in your mind that you can give to Jesus? He wants His perfect love and Presence to fill our minds and free us from the enemies attacks!

ONLINE ALTERATION: Lasso challenge! Invite children to gather a piece of string, shoelace or floss. Give them 1 minute to try and create a lasso from what they have. When they have finished, show off your creations. Ask them to find an object nearby and try to lasso it. Can they hold that object captive with their lasso? Read **2 Corinthians 10:5** Talk about what it means to ask Jesus to take thoughts captive. Which thoughts would He keep? Which would he cast out?

SUPPLIES: *none*

We are going to play "toolbox charades". Take turns acting out one object that could be found in a toolbox. Take turns guessing what it is.

(Example: hammer, screwdriver, measuring tape, safety goggles, nail)

When you are finished, discuss how God gives us the tools we need to fight against the enemy's attacks. What are those tools? Can a handyman do his job without having the right tools in his toolbox? What if he only had tissues, cups, and spoons in his toolbox? In the same way we need to be sure that we have all the tools we need to stand against the enemies attacks. When we do, **2 Corinthians 10:5** reminds us that we can demolish every proud or bad thought that the enemy tries to attack us with!

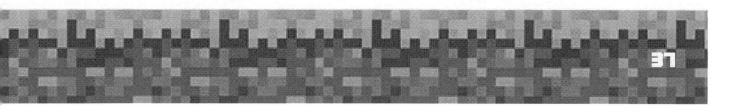

FIVE. TIME TO TRAVEL

WARRANTY: GOD WILL LEAD ME

BEFORE YOU BEGIN
This section is for you - the grown ups!
You are welcome to also read with the children.

So Minecraft is a family affair at our house. My 4 year old daughter did not want to be left out of the adventure. She quickly learned how to build and battle. But one thing I love about her, is that she is always thinking about others. She was playing with her brother and cousin and was building this enormous tower to the sky. I was like "Chandler, what are you doing? That's not going to be a good house for living in." She said, "It's not a house, it's a tall tower so that way, if anyone gets lost, they can find their way back." I hope that no matter where you find yourself in your spiritual life (whether you are far from God, questioning God, unsure about God, mad at God or indifferent), that you will know you can always come back to the Cross. Your life is never too far gone or messed up to "hit respawn."

Melissa

Growing up I always thought **Genesis 1-3** was about Adam and Eve eating a bad fruit. It reminded me of Snow White eating the poisoned apple. If only Eve had not eaten the bad fruit, we would all be living completely different lives right now. I like to also think this is why I trust chocolate more than my fruits and veggies. I mean can you really trust a food that looks like a tree?

Here is the thing though, the story in Genesis is not about the fruit but about choosing to walk away from God's will in our lives. The evil was not in the fruit but in the justifications of Adam and Eve's hearts and minds. Do we trust God? Is living in His will what drives us each day? Or is it something else?

When we follow after God, He has a will for our lives that will lead us into great adventures. God created us. He placed desires and dreams within each one of us. Many of those dreams can only be fully discovered with the help of His Holy Spirit at work inside of us. God has the power to sift through every doubt and every lie to find those precious dreams buried deep within our identities.

The secret is, we can only discover them if we trust Him to lead the way. Are you trusting God to lead you today? I challenge you to take every thought that comes your way today and ask God to take it. If it is within His will, ask the Holy Spirit to let it stay. If it is against His will, trust God to take it away. Walking against His call on your life will only keep you from your greatest adventures. Be ready for Him to uncover unforgiveness, hurts, and even shame that He wants to free you from.

We are praying for you and excited for the victories God has in store for your life! It's time to travel - let's let God lead us.

Amy

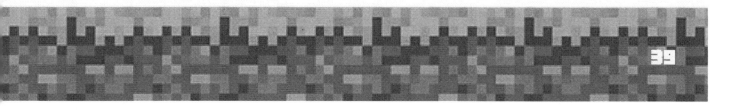

QUEST TIME

Mapping out your quest through question and discussion

OPERATIONS MANUAL

God's Word maps out how our faith will help us see great adventures. In games we can use maps and portals to travel to incredible places. We may face unknown lands or even new enemies but remember if we follow after God He will always lead us!

Option: Get out scrap paper and something to write with for each child.

Press Pause: We are going to take a minute to stop doing anything for 60 seconds. During this time write down all the thoughts that go through your mind. Write down any feelings you have.

When the time is up, invite the children to share some of their thoughts. How many thoughts did they have? What were they about?

How often do you think about God during that time?
How much do you think about God- or the things of God- during each day?

Read **Psalm 1:2**

Who here thinks about God day and night? Some versions of this verse say "think about God's law" or "God's teaching" day and night. Your mind is like a chest that holds your inventory. In our apps and games, we hold onto items we want and need as inventory. We can build a chest to hold even more items.

Read **Matthew 6:21**

The Bible says 'where your treasure is, is where your heart is.' In other words, what we keep in our chest of treasured inventory, will tell others what is important to us. What thoughts fill up your mind? If we take inventory of what we spend time thinking about, we can tell where our treasure is.

> Now that we have taken inventory of our thoughts, we can get ready to travel!

Option: Play a packing game where you race to pack up a luggage or chest with items to travel. Label items with words that worship God and worries, fears, or doubts that keep us from God. Give children a certain amount of time to "pack" their travel chests/luggage with only the inventory that will keep their minds focused on God.

Talking about baptism:

When we accept Jesus into our lives... when we let Him lead... He gives us His Holy Spirit. The Holy Spirit is God in us.

Romans 8:11 The Spirit of the God who raised Jesus from the dead is living in you. So the God who raised Christ from the dead will also give life to your bodies. He will do this because of his Spirit who lives in you.

God loves us so much that He wants to travel WITH us. God doesn't just live in Heaven. He gives us His Holy Spirit to live in us and give us new life- sending us on new adventures with Him! If you want to know more about God living with you and leading you, ask your leaders about what it means to be baptized and accept Jesus as your Savior! Accepting Jesus, is what opens the door for God to live in us and with us- today and forever. Read **John 14:6**

Have you ever been to a museum or park and seen a tour guide? What are tour guides? Sometimes there are tour guides who are also translating for people who speak a different language. Have you ever visited a store and had someone walk up to your parents and show you where everything is?

Read **John 14:16**

Bigger than a museum, park, or store- God made the whole world! Living with His Holy Spirit in us is like living with the greatest tour guide within us. He knows where everything is, why it's there, and how we can live our best lives. That is why He can take us on the greatest adventures! In our games and apps, we can build portals to travel to unknown places. There are a handful of different portals you can travel to in the game but in each one, you find new resources, sometimes bigger enemies and more beautiful worlds.

How are portals like the Holy Spirit? When our bodies are filled with the Holy Spirit, we have access to new heavenly resources, seeing our world as God does and it gives us the ability to conquer new, deeper battles.

Do you find it hard to both hear and listen to God's word? What can make that difficult?

Read **Psalm 37:4-6**

What do you desire? Reflect on your commitment and trust in the Lord. Only when we desire God above anything else can we begin claiming those new places, resources, and experiences. God loves you and wants to satisfy you more than anything we desire that is apart from Him.

Here is an example: I used to think peanut butter brownie fudge ice cream was my favorite ice-cream flavor. I would tell everyone that there was no flavor I desired more! I was confident that in order for me to enjoy ice cream it had to be this flavor! Until… one day I visited a friend who took me to a new ice cream store. I had never been there before and would have never visited it without her. She was my guide and I trusted her. She knew me and she also knew the place we traveled to better than I did. So I was willing to trust her. That place had the best ice cream I have ever tasted! I am so glad I followed and trusted her! I now have experienced a great adventure, greater ice cream, and discovered I have different desires. I am forever changed.

How can this story remind us of God?

It's a silly (true) story but it gives us an example of how God is with us! He wants to lead us on great adventures to taste greater things! Following God will leave us forever changed!

> Pray that God would align your desires with His. Pray for your trust to be sharpened and strengthened in Him.

PRAYER: ASSEMBLY REQUIRED

Building up our minds by breaking down one Bible verse and praying it together.

STEP 1:
Read **Colossians 3:2**

STEP 2:
Talk about it together:

> Where do you spend most of your time?
> What is the first thing you think about every day when you wake up?
> What is the last thing you think about before falling asleep?
> What do you think about the most during the day?

STEP 3:
Think about it: It can be difficult to keep God first in our life if we don't make time for Him. Let's take a minute and think about how we can set our minds on things above so we can begin building.

STEP 3:
Reflect on things that you have placed before God. Can we ever see the goodness of God if we don't first think about how good He is? How can we hear from God if we don't first set our hearts and minds on listening to Him?
FOR OLDER KIDS: *Read James 4:8*

STEP 4:
Pray about some ways we can set our minds on things "above" instead of "earthly" things.

OFF SCREEN CHALLENGES

Troubleshooting what you are learning; interactive activities for real life mode together.

SUPPLIES: *none*

Play *Follow the Leader*. Play one round normal. Play another round, with a new leader, this time everyone has to follow the leader WITHOUT looking at him or her. For younger kids, give them a specific place to look at - like their shirts! Try following the leader while looking at yourself. Is it easy or hard to follow someone you are not looking at? Read **Colossians 3:2.** When we "set our minds on heavenly things" or "things above" we are looking at God. When we "set our minds on earthly things" it is as silly as looking at our shirts in our game! If we want to follow God, we have to keep our thoughts focused on Him! Continue this discussion with specific stories and examples or play the game again. You could play and tell everyone to follow the leader but call out earthly things for them to keep their eyes fixed on.

For example: Play a round but keep eyes fixed on the wall - this represents minds fixed, focused and filled with worries. Discuss "earthly" worries that can fill our minds and keep us from being focused on God. Play another round but keep eyes fixed on your own shoes- this represents minds fixed on what I want and where I want to go. Discuss how difficult it is to keep our minds ready to hear what God wants when we are focused on always getting what we want. The game is always easier when we can focus our eyes and minds on the leader!

SUPPLIES: paper or rocks, pencils or markers, journals and printed verse to make prompts for each prayer station for off screen challenge

Work with your youth group, family or friends to create a prayer walk. Maybe your leader could organize this as a hike or maybe this is something you could do with a group of students around your school track. You could also designate 4 areas for each prompt. Lay out 4 prompts along the walk to read, reflect and take action in your life for each prompt. We would love for you to share how you set up your prayer walk! Don't forget to tag us and share your ideas!

SET UP A "PRAYER WALK" WITH FOUR STATIONS. INVITE CHILDREN TO VISIT EACH STATION AND INTERACT WITH WHAT IS THERE.

Station One: Surrender.
Have something the student/kids can write a problem or area of their life they haven't fully surrendered to God. (They could write it on paper and pin it to the cross, they could write it on a rock and lay it at the feet of the cross). Read **Psalm 55:22.** Pray for God to help you surrender the things that are keeping you heavy.

Station Two: Peace.
Have something students/kids can pick up that symbolizes peace. (It could be a new journal to write in or a keepsake). Read **Philippians 4:7 & Zephaniah 3:17.** Pray that you will know and experience the peace of God. Pray for God to calm your fears.

Station Three: Direction.
Have students/kids reflect on the direction of their life. Are they going in the direction that God would want them to go? Are they going in circles? Have they hit a roadblock or feel stuck? Read Psalm 32:8. Pray that God will make it clear to you, the best pathway for your life. Pray for His guidance and protection over your steps.

Station Four: Protection.
Have students/kids reflect on where they are seeking refuge and strength from. Are they pulling from Kingdom resources or worldly resources? Read **Psalm 46:1, Romans 8:37-38 & Deuteronomy 31:6**. Pray for God to be your refuge and your strength in times of trouble. Pray that you would operate from a place of victory in Christ and if you haven't given your life to Christ yet, consider the gift God is offering to you.

SIX SKIP SPECTATOR MODE
WARRANTY: IT'S TIME TO START MY FAITH

BEFORE YOU BEGIN
This section is for you - the grown ups!
You are welcome to also read with the children.

In "spectator mode," there's no plan, purpose or access to resources. I think we sometimes like the idea of spectator mode because it eliminates responsibility or accountability, but we miss out on the fullness of God when we are just an observer. God is asking us to actively participate in community with Him. I have seen my son try and observe his cousin playing Minecraft and it's so difficult for him to not want to give some advice, tell his cousin what to do, or take the device from him so he can play. We were not designed to live in spectator mode. Think about it. From the beginning, God was actively engaged in community with the son and the Holy Spirit, creating the universe! And now the Holy Spirit is active, living, working, moving through us Jesus is telling us if we love Him then we will feed his sheep (His people). **John 21:15-17.**

Melissa

When I first saw my husband, I was not in love. (Melissa can attest that this is true.) We were in high school at that time. At the wise age of 17, I was a skeptical spectator of guys. While sure, many of them looked good, I was not about to invite them into my world. Needless to say, years later he won me over. I shed my spectator mode and decided to marry this man.

These games we play on our apps give us options for what mode we want for our lives. The modes determine how we interact with the world we live in. God gives us that same free will in our lives. Many of us begin our life of faith based on a feeling.

It reminds me of that honeymoon love that convinces us to marry someone we receive butterflies from. I heard it once said, "Falling in love is easy. It's staying in love that is difficult." I fell in love with my husband a few years after first seeing him. The excitement of that honeymoon love was short lived but the love I have for him now grew only after choosing to stand by him even after the butterflies flew off.

Every grown up knows, feelings fade. It can be easy to only follow our feelings when it comes to any relationship- especially our relationship with God. When we feel like living by faith we reach out for God but when the feelings fade we step back into spectator mode. This is called "consumerism christianity." We follow our faith when it feeds us and we like what we receive from it but our spiritual growth is stunted when we "don't like what God's Word is selling."

> We stop trusting and obeying. We refuse to stand by the God
> we once felt such adoration for.

This gospel unveils a continual revelation of God's righteousness—a perfect righteousness given to us when we believe. And it moves us from receiving life through faith, to the power of living by faith. This is what the Scripture means when it says:

"We are right with God through life-giving faith!" - Romans 1:17 TPT

Living with God is meant to include a continual revelation of God's righteousness. This revelation from God can only occur in our lives when we choose to stand by him and not on the sidelines like spectators. When we keep reading **Romans 1**, we see how this relationship started with receiving life through faith. Most of us began our faith because of the love, joy or hope that we received in our life when we first fell in love with God. Or maybe we say someone else who had something in their life we wanted. So, we visited their church. We committed to try and follow God because of what we received from Him. This is where we get consumerism Christianity- a love and a faith based on what we can get. We have the same potential to base our commitment in marriage relationships based on those same feelings.

But, in order to receive that continual revelation of God's {right-ness & goodness in our lives} we must move from receiving life through faith to the power of living BY faith. We will miss out in life, if we never choose to stand by our faith when feelings fade. That is where the life-giving power is ound. The power that gives us life changing revelations of hope, love, contentment, identity, and joy.

I loved my husband on our wedding day. Like most 20 year olds, I loved the feelings I received from him when those butterflies came. Our love has grown only because I committed to the power of living by faith in marriage. When the feelings I once received flew away, my faith provided the power and revelation I needed to love this man. Sure, we have lived seasons where running back to the sidelines seemed like the solution. Loving hurts. Trusting is tiring. And living out our faith in our own power can feel impossible. I thank God for the continual revelation that my life is not meant to be lived as a spectator who always receives. I was created to live by HIS life giving power. Like we discussed a few lessons back, He wants to be the foundation that I build every part of my life upon.

I want to encourage you today to keep building. Maybe hurt stopped you. Maybe someone left and you ran back to the sidelines. Maybe you are building but are weary today. You are not alone. God gives us life-giving faith. A faith based on the love He showed us in sending Jesus. You and I don't have to earn this love. Like a bride standing before her groom. He is there with you- watching you in adoration of your beauty and strength. He desires you. Have faith. God wants not only for you to receive his love but to choose it as the foundation you live by. Skip spectator mode, ya'll! Press start on your faith today and move from receiving bits of faith to living BY faith. You are not alone. God is partnering with you.

Amy

QUEST TIME

Mapping out your quest through question and discussion

OPERATIONS MANUAL

Spectator mode is a gamemode that allows the player to fly around and observe the world without interacting with it in any way. Jesus isn't looking for spectators. He is looking for active faith. Let's get in the game and press start. Let's activate living out our faith!

Are there moments where you feel like you are in spectator mode in your spiritual life?

> Think of the word ACTIVATE.

What words do you hear in this one word ACTIVATE? Break those words down. What do they mean? When we activate a character in a game, we make them ACT or become ACTIVE by INTERACTING with people and places around them.

How can we ACTIVATE our faith?

Can you ever start a game without ACTIVATING a character? Would that fun be fun or boring?

God has great adventures for us but we have to have active faith- meaning we have to act based on what we believe! How can we start living in this mode? How can we start activating our faith in our minds and with our thoughts?

When we are in spectator mode in our life, we are missing out on God adventures! What are God adventures? What do you think they might be?

Has there ever been a skill, sport, or hobby you really wanted to learn? *Share a personal story.*

Here is a fun example: If I want to be a chef what can I do?
>Maybe watch some videos of amazing chefs
>Maybe follow amazing chefs on social media
>Maybe practice recipes again and again at home
>Maybe spend time and money to invest in what I need to grow as a chef and begin my culinary adventures

It's not enough to just watch a video about it and automatically think you're an expert. And this is true in our spiritual lives. If you and I want to go on adventures with God and grow as His disciples what can we do? It's important to note to students that "the doing" is not our salvation. It's not the thing that saves us. We get off spectator mode because of Jesus' amazing doing; it is out of gratitude that we do things.

Faith is ACTIVE!

Read **Romans 2:13**

Here is a good version we can read from the International Childrens' Bible (ICB):

Hearing the law does not make people right with God. The law makes people right with God only if they obey what the law says. Romans 2:13 ICB

What does this verse tell us?
Does God want us to just hear about Him or do what His words say?
God wants us to be both hearers and doers of His word.

What does it mean to believe in God?
Did you know that angels and demons believe in God too?

Read **James 2:19-20**

God says, when we choose to only believe in him we are "fools." Our faith is "worth nothing" if we only believe in Him. God doesn't just want us to believe Him. He wants us to trust, follow, and obey Him.

How can we trust, follow, and obey God?

Option: Call out example scenarios where children would have the choice to trust, follow and obey God. Explain the scenario and invite the children to answer how they could act our their faith by trusting, following, and obeying God.

Example 1: During recess, the boys on the field yell at me that I kicked the ball wrong. They call me names and hurt my feelings. I want to yell back at them…
How can I ACT?

Example 2: My teacher told me not to talk but I really want to tell my best friend what happened yesterday at my house. It's a really funny story. My teacher just left the room and no one is around… How can I ACT?

Example 3: My little brother just hit me! I know I am not supposed to hit back but he really deserves to feel what it's like when someone hits him. I wouldn't hit him too hard… How can I ACT?

Can you think of other examples?

Do you like math? Did you know that all of your favorite games are created through math? Through mathematical equations, the men and women who built your favorite games were able to code and create them! Here is a fun math
equation that explains what we are talking about today:

FAITH = BELIEVE + ACT
or
FAITH = BELIEVE + (TRUST, FOLLOW, OBEY)

In the math class, algebra, we would learn that whatever is written on either side of the equation (= sign) is of equal value. In order to have faith, we must believe and act. How do we ACT on our faith? We TRUST, FOLLOW, and OBEY God.

Press Pause: Let's talk about bullies. How do we act like spectators sometimes when we see a kid being bullied? How can we act on our faith when we see someone being bullied? God does not want us to live in spectator mode. He can use you if you choose to trust, follow, and obey him.

Read **Matthew 16:24**

Here is a good version we can read from the International Childrens' Bible (ICB):

> **Then Jesus said to his followers, "If anyone wants to follow me, he must say 'no' to the things he wants. He must be willing even to die on a cross, and he must follow me. Matthew 16:24 ICB**

What did Jesus mean?

Have you ever wanted to do something that you knew God didn't want you to do?
Share stories. Jesus wants us to say "no" to the things that we want to do if they are not what He wants. (For example: hitting my little brother when he makes me mad or ignoring my parents when they ask me to help).

Did Jesus want to die on the cross?
Jesus was *willing* to die on a cross because He *wanted* to obey God.

How would our lives be changed if Jesus stayed in spectator mode?
(no Holy Spirit in us and no promise of Heaven).

> Jesus refused to live in spectator mode.
> Because of His faith in action,
> because He obeyed God
> even to the point of dying in a cross,
> we can be with God today and forever!

FOR OLDER KIDS: *Jesus is looking for disciples; followers. And I'm not talking about the kind of followers people get on social media. Jesus says in order to be His follower, we have to put down some things. Now Jesus isn't saying go sell all your stuff if you want to follow Him. But to the rich ruler in Matthew 19:21, his possessions were more important than Jesus. That's why Jesus asked him to put the possessions down. And Christ is saying to us. The things you put before me- put them down- so that I can lead you. We cannot remain in Him if we are remaining in the things that distract us from Him. When we remain in Christ, we don't attach our identity to anything other than Him. True identity is found in Christ! It can be fun to create your own identity in the game. But think of all the wonderful and beautiful things God wants for you outside of spectator mode!*

Read Habakkuk 2:4

What is God's promise to those who live out their faith? Remember, we can only live the adventure God created for us when we begin to trust Him with every thought.

PRAYER: ASSEMBLY REQUIRED

Building up our minds by breaking down one Bible verse and praying it together.

STEP 1:
Read **James 1:22** (Here is the International Children's Bible version:)

Do what God's teaching says; do not just listen and do nothing. When you only sit and listen, you are fooling yourselves.

STEP 2:
What word do you hear repeated 3 times? Why is it repeated?

STEP 3:
To "only sit & listen" to God is foolish, what would it mean if we "do what God's teaching says?"

STEP 4:
Can I "do" what someone says if I don't "listen" to them?

STEP 5:
Have you ever gone on a family adventure? Who or what do your parent's listen to, in order to go on the adventure? A map on a phone or in the car? How much fun would your adventure be if you only looked at the map, sat there, did nothing, but just listened to where the map told you to go? No fun!

STEP 6:
Know that God loves you! He has fun adventures for you and me. We can only experience those adventures when we "do" what His word tells us- activating our faith. And with active faith, we can go on so many adventures with God!

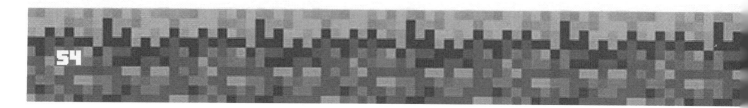

OFF SCREEN CHALLENGES

Troubleshooting what you are learning; interactive activities for real life mode together.

SUPPLIES: hat, shoes, jacket, a belt, a Bible, and a lid for off screen challenge

The floor is LAVA! If you haven't seen this game before, it's super fun! Create your own obstacle course using pillows and living room furniture to get from one side of the house to the other. You can only advance by collecting all pieces of armor throughout your journey:

Have a hat or helmet to represent the **"helmet of salvation"**
Have a pair of shoes to represent the **"readiness to share the gospel"**
Have a shirt or jacket to represent the **"breastplate of God's righteousness"**
Have a belt to represent **"God's truth"**
Have a Bible to represent **"His word-the sword"**
Have a lid to represent **"the shield of faith"**

If you or a teammate drops an item on the way on the floor, you must all start over. If you or a teammate touches the ground, the whole team must start over. Let the adventure begin! We would love for you to share how you set up your LAVA course! Don't forget to tag us and share your ideas! This would be a great time to implement our study song and practice **the Armor of God (QR CODE in the back of the book).**

SUPPLIES: *none*

Play **Simon Says**. In the middle of the game tell the kids "simon says do nothing" and then sit for about 1 minute. Kids will become anxious, moan and groan.

Ask: Does doing nothing make the game fun?

Play again this time everytime you say "simon says" only have the children watch you do things. For example "simon, says watch me spin in circles... simon says, watch me eat this cookie... simon says, watch me dance..."

Ask: Does just watching me make the game fun? What makes this game fun? Read **James 1:22**

God wants us to have a lot of fun adventures in our lives. Just like in our game, God wants us to not just listen to Him or watch Him but to live out life with Him and God's Kingdom in mind. Let's play our game again but this time you can DO what Simon says. This game is a fun reminder that God wants us to activate our faith and DO what He says!

SUPPLIES: Long/large Mirrors, tape, construction paper, crayons or colored pencils
(Tape two pieces of construction paper onto the mirror with 1-2 feet in between them.) Invite two children to look into the mirror. Position the children where half of their faces are covered up by the piece of papers taped onto the mirror. Invite them, while looking at the half reflections in the mirror to draw the half of their face they can't see on the taped paper. Give them 1-2 minutes to do this and then set up the activity again for another set of children to participate.

Read **James 1:22-23** Do what God's teaching says; do not just listen and do nothing. When you only sit and listen, you are fooling yourselves. A person who hears God's teaching and does nothing is like a man looking in a mirror.

Read **Corinthians 13:12** For now we see only a reflection as in a mirror; then we shall see face to face. Now I know in part; then I shall know fully, even as I am fully known.

When we act on our faith, it helps us to remember who God is and how good God is. Actions help us remember. *(This is also why your school teachers and sports coaches don't just tell you how to do something- they also have you try and do it on your own).* When we only listen- we will forget. The partial mirror is like our life with God. Right now we can only see glimpses or partial reflections of God. We don't always know what He is doing or see how things will work out but one day we will know the whole plan. We will be able to see Him fully- with nothing to get in the way of our view. Can you imagine what that day will be like?

ONLINE ALTERATION: While on your video lesson, show your face and then cover it. Ask the children about something on your face. *For example:* what color are my eyes? How many freckles do I have? What color are my earrings? Call out a few children to then repeat this. After you have done this a few times, continue with the conversation & Bible verses above.

SEVEN. BUILDING BIGGER THINGS

WARRANTY: I COME ALIVE IN GOD'S KINGDOM

BEFORE YOU BEGIN
This section is for you - the grown ups!
You are welcome to also read with the children.

So my nephew was spawning zombie eggs in the game "just to see what would happen." It didn't end well. And it wasn't like he accidentally did it. He went into his inventory, sought out the egg, placed it in a dark cave, it grew and obviously, in survival, those things aren't built to assist but to destroy. We can't expect to reap good in our lives if we intentionally spawn evil.

In **Galatians 6:7,** God's Word states, **"Do not be deceived, God is not mocked; for whatever a man sows, this he will also reap;"** sow meaning "put into" and reap meaning "get out of." Did you notice how Galatians 6:7 begins? It says, **"Do not be deceived, God is not mocked."** Here, we see the "root" cause for what we reap (get). Deception; not understanding God's law or thinking you're above it is what sows destruction in our lives. You wouldn't expect to spawn a zombie egg and get a dolphin?! But for some reason we are surprised in our life when bad behavior = bad consequences.

"Why are you spawning evil eggs I don't understand?" This is a question I asked my 10 year old nephew. And do you know what his answer was? "I don't know, I was just curious." We must be careful with our curiosity. It can be a tool the enemy uses in our life to get us to sin. Satan used it in the garden with Adam and Eve and he is still using it today. We are constantly in a tug-a-war with our flesh (inclination toward sin) and the spirit (the desire to be in the light with Christ). And sometimes the flesh in us says it's okay, just look at the endermen. But don't let your curiosity keep you from the beautiful things God wants to give you!

Melissa

QUEST TIME

Mapping out your quest through question and discussion

OPERATIONS MANUAL

Let's open up God's Word together and take a look at how we can come alive in God's Kingdom! Living in God's Kingdom is greater than any life we can build on our own.

Read **John 10:10**

We talked about how the enemy is like a thief but who is the person speaking? Jesus.
Why did Jesus say he came to earth?
What does Jesus want to give us?
Does that mean a life without Jesus isn't full?

Option: Get out a snack, drink, or treat. Tell everyone they can have a snack (or drink) but you do not want to give them the full snack. If you have a cup for them to drink, pour most of it out and then hand them a cup with a few sips in it. If you are passing out a snack or treat, break off a large chunk, and only pass out small pieces of the snack. Ask the children if they enjoyed what you gave them? Did they get the full snack? No. In the same way, we can live without Jesus but when we do we are settling for pieces. God wants us to enjoy the fullness of life- not just pieces!

The Keys to the Kingdom

Read **John 14:6**

If God has a huge Kingdom that gives us heavenly resources- how do we get in? Jesus is our key! Jesus unlocks the kingdom gate so we can be with God and begin living a full life with Him now! *(Remind children about our discussion from Lesson 5 about following Jesus and baptism.)*

Read **1 Peter 3:18**

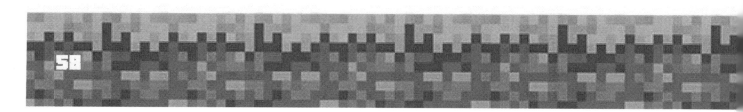

One big way we can begin our adventures with Jesus is by letting His Holy Spirit make us alive! What does that mean? This means that we can invite the Holy Spirit to search our minds and hearts and remove any fears, lies, and doubts that keep us from Jesus. We can invite Him to replace old "dead" thoughts with new thoughts that bring us closer to Him. He will renew our minds with:

- Hope instead of doubt
- Love instead of fear
- Joy instead of pain
- Peace instead of anger
- Patience instead of worries
- Kindness instead of loneliness
- Goodness instead of unforgiveness
- Self Control instead of panic
- Contentment instead of sadness

Read **Galatians 5:22-23**

What are some fruits of the Spirit?

If you see a tree outside, how can you tell what kind of tree it is? If it is a fruiting tree, one simple way to tell what tree it is would be by what fruit is hanging from it's branches.
Will an orange tree ever have pineapples hanging from it's branches?
Will an oak tree ever have pears hanging from it?

In the same way, we cannot have those fruits from the Holy Spirit without inviting Him to live in us. He has to be planted in us before we can bear His fruit.

FOR OLDER KIDS: *Read Matthew 7:18*

This reminds me of spawning in our apps and games. What is spawning? Can you spawn a sheep from a zombie egg? How does that relate to our Bible verse? What does your spiritual fruit look like? Are you spawning good thoughts in your life?

> Without Jesus we Lose the Game

God is without error and sinless. Perfect. No evil, sadness, or selfishness exists around him. Because we sin, we are separated from God.

Read **Ephesians 2:1**

Our sin separates us from God. Game over. God is love. Anything apart from God is darkness and without love. Dead. Because God is love, He doesn't give up on us when we sin. He sent us Jesus. When we choose to follow Jesus, we can re-spawn in life. We can leave our old, dead, sinful life behind and follow Jesus.

Have you heard the story of Frankenstein? Was Frankenstein a new creation or a monster? A monster. Why? His creator used old things to piece together his creation. In the end he made a monster who came to life- not new life. When we choose to follow Jesus we have to let go of the old parts of us- thoughts and desires that keep us from God. Jesus doesn't want us to life where we smell like rotten flesh, stitched together with broken pieces and a cloudy dumb brain. He loves us so much more! He wants to give you new life!

Jesus has many names (Lamb of God, Lord of Lords..etc)

He is also called the King of Kings. What does that name mean? He is the one King with power and authority greater than any other king.

Read **Revelation 17:14**

Anyone can wage war and try to fight Jesus, the King of Kings. What does this verse say will happen? He will triumph and win! Jesus is victorious over every old, bad, evil, and misguided enemy attack. The best part of this verse says He will not claim the victory alone. Who is He bringing with him? Us! His followers.

> We win when we choose to follow Jesus!

The Winning Build:

The Pharisee asked, "Teacher, which command in the law is the most important?" Jesus answered, "'Love the Lord your God with all your heart, soul and mind.' This is the first and most important command. And the second command is like the first: 'Love your neighbor as you love yourself.' All the law and the writings of the prophets depend on these two commands." Matthew 11:36-40

We build our best life when our number one goal is to love God with heart, soul, mind and strength. This means we make sure that every desire and thought we have involved God's love.

AND we cannot win in life without loving others and ourselves!

In games we can create new characters if we make a mistake as creators or if we get tired of the original characters we made. God doesn't make mistakes! You are no mistake. God could create you but He doesn't because:

**He created you on purpose, He loves you, and He has a purpose for you.
God doesn't want you to be any other character.
He wants you to be you!**

Sometimes we believe lies that God wants us to be like Jesus but this verse reminds us that he wants us to LOVE Jesus! God is not waiting for you to be perfect. He knows you and loves you today. He wants to be a part of your adventure today. As you choose to love Him more you will watch your character gain those heavenly abilities. With God we can win, we can explore new adventures, and create some of the greatest builds ever!
Fix your thoughts on that. **#MINDcraft**

For Older Kids: *Read 2 Corinthians 5:17*

What are the "old" and "new" this verse talks about? Is it possible for us to have old thoughts and habits even after we choose to follow Jesus?

Have you ever had a snack in your hand but dropped it on the ground?
Have you ever dropped one on a dirty ground? How many of you thought of picking back up that old nasty snack? Tell the truth!

When we choose to follow Jesus, there are some thoughts and habits we need to drop. Will we be tempted to pick back up those old habits? Absolutely! But remember, if our hands, hearts and heads are filled with the old - we won't be able to be filled with the new life Jesus wants for us.

Have you ever built a character in your games that you later chose to demolish? Why? Do you have habits and thoughts from your "old" character that need to be demolished? What thoughts and ideas keep us from fully trusting Jesus? These thoughts are like cracks that weaken our builds.

Read Hebrews 12:1

When we think about HOW we build, we need to consider who we are surrounded by. In Hebrews, Paul starts by encouraging us to have a community of accountability then he is telling us to throw off everything that hinders us. That's intentional demolition!

Our faith in Jesus Christ moves us to a place of surrendering our old inventory and turning to His Holy Spirit to create a new life in us. Take a minute to take inventory of your life. Ask God to help reveal to you the thoughts and voices in your life that need to be demolished in order for you to craft your mind to be a new character in Jesus.

PRAYER: ASSEMBLY REQUIRED

Building up our minds by breaking down one Bible verse and praying it together.

STEP 1:
Read **Matthew 6:10**

This verse comes from a prayer Jesus prayed.
Jesus started his prayer like this to show us how we can pray.

STEP 2:
Whose Kingdom is this verse talking about? Gods! What does that tell us about God? He is a King! The Bible tells us Jesus is called "King of Kings" *(meaning He is the King who is stronger than any other king).* God's Kingdom is Jesus' Kingdom.

STEP 3:
What does it mean to pray and say "[Jesus'] Kingdom to come"? When we invite Jesus' Kingdom into our lives, we agree to make Him King.

STEP 4:
Inviting King Jesus' Kingdom to "come" into our lives will:

1. Cover our hearts and minds with His Love that will give us victory over EVERY enemy.
2. His Presence will lead us to Truth.
3. Faith in Him protects us. Because of King Jesus, the Holy Spirit can drive out darkness and sadness.
4. Give us access to the most powerful Kingdom- A Kingdom that gives us hope when other kingdoms fail around us.
5. Provide an army from heaven! Jesus' Kingdom has an army. His army is angels.

STEP 5:

"Your will be done" means that you are trusting Jesus to be King of your thoughts and actions. You will do what He desires, not always what you desire.

STEP 6:

Will you choose Jesus as King? Will you invite him today to bring His Kingdom into your life? To do as He "wills"?

Spend time in quiet. Be still before God. Invite children to pray this memory verse in their minds and hearts. Invite Jesus to be King. Thank Him for His heavenly Kingdom that he is willing to give us because He loves us! Thank God for the victory He is bringing into our lives- even the victories we cannot see yet.

OFF SCREEN CHALLENGES

Troubleshooting what you are learning; interactive activities for real life mode together.

SUPPLIES: paper, pencils, markers, crayons for off screen challenge

Create a new egg for each fruit of the spirit listed in **Galatians 5:22-23**. Draw them out, giving each one unique colors and instructions for use. Don't forget to share your creative eggs with us! You could also get some real eggs to decorate if you're feeling extra creative!

Please tag us or send pictures of them to us! Happy hatching! **#MINDcraft**

SUPPLIES: Plastic Easter Eggs, fill each colored egg with either good/bad items (or pictures)

Hide the eggs around the room. Invite children to find them and open them. Compare the items you find. Did the blue eggs have good or bad things in them? What about the pink eggs?

In our apps and games we can collect eggs and spawn different creatures.
Another way to say it, is that these eggs allow players to create new life. God wants to create new life for us. He wants to spawn His promises in our life. He wants to spawn thoughts that lead us to His Truth and Love.

Galatians 5:22-23 reminds us that God wants to spawn the good things from His Spirit living in us. We cannot receive this new life if we hold onto bad eggs. What are some bad eggs you are holding onto? (lies, anger, fears, doubts...) Pray
together for God to take those bad eggs and invite Him to bring new life to the thoughts in your mind. Thank Him for loving you so much that He cares about
every single thought you keep!

Hide the eggs and play.

ONLINE ALTERATION: Use the same supplies but only one egg of each color. Invite one child to be "it." They have to walk away from the camera for 30 seconds. When they do, invite the children to pick one of the eggs filled with a "bad" item.

Put all the good eggs in a pile but add the one bad one.

When the child who is "it" returns tell them to call out which colored egg they want to spawn. Tell them that all the eggs are good eggs except for one. As they call out colors, open the corresponding egg.

Give them 1 point for each egg they choose that ends up being good but their turn is oven once you open the bad egg.

When the open the bad egg the other children call out somethings like "rotten egg" or "zombie egg."

When you are done talk about how each egg represents our thoughts. Some thoughts in our mind are bad eggs! We can hold onto lies or fears or anger that keeps us from getting close to God and feeling the fruits of His Spirit in us. How can we tell if a thought is from God or not? A good thought or a bad thought?

Pray together for God to take those bad eggs and invite Him to bring new life to the thoughts in your mind.

Thank Him for loving you so much that He cares about every single thought you keep!

This QR code links to the instrumental, lyrics and the version with vocals for

STANDING IN THE ARMOR

the MindCraft original Children's Praise Song.

HOW TO USE A QR CODE

1. Open the camera app on your phone.
2. Scan the QR code above until you see a link with pop up.
3. Click the link. It will open up a link to song files in dropbox.
4. Enjoy!

Check out more fun resources from Melissa Sheridan and Amy Traurig by scanning these QR codes!

SPOOKTACULAR
4 week curriculum

Saved by the Bell
4 week curriculum

PILLAGE
Pirate Curriculum & BONUS
Activities for Sea Saul Shipwreck

PIRATES
SEA SAUL'S SHIPWRECK

Children's Musical PLUS Over 40 Hours Of Children's Curriculum!

Digital Download   Curriculum E-Book & Print   Script E-Book & Print

Looking for more? Be sure to find us on Amazon, Facebook, and teacherspayteachers.com.

Made in the USA
Columbia, SC
17 May 2023

16869246R00041